T0078378

THE LIES MY
DAUGHTER
TOLD

A Mother's Account

ESTHER JAMES

WESTBOW
PRESS®
A DIVISION OF THOMAS NELSON
& ZONDERVAN

WestBow Press books may be ordered through booksellers or by contacting:

WestBow Press
A Division of Thomas Nelson & Zondervan
1663 Liberty Drive
Bloomington, IN 47403
www.westbowpress.com
844-714-3454

Scripture taken from the New King James Version® Copyright © 1982 by Thomas Nelson. Used by permission. All rights reserved.

Library of Congress Control Number: 2021900272

ISBN: 978-1-6642-1858-1 (sc)
ISBN: 978-1-6642-1859-8 (e)

Print information available on the last page.

WestBow Press rev. date: 1/20/2021

TABLE OF CONTENTS

ACKNOWLEDGMENT

I WOULD LIKE TO EXPRESS my gratitude to God, who is the head of my life. My eyes look to the hills from which comes my help. "My help comes from the Lord, Who made the heaven and earth" (Psalm 121:1-2 NKJV). Since I was a little girl, I knew that God had his hands on me and favored me.

God gave me the creative ideas to write this book along with another book *Doing God's Will: My Memoir* during the 2020 pandemic. God gives us the power to get wealth.

I dedicate this book to my daughter, who is the subject of this book, in addition to my son and grandchildren. I pray that they all will receive salvation and have a relationship with God.

INTRODUCTION

HAVE YOU EVER MET A person who consistently told lies? The storylines are so good that you contemplate in your mind if he or she is telling the truth. How do our children expect us to believe them when they constantly lie? As a parent, how can you support your child if they lie to you? Since my daughter was old enough to talk, she has been telling lies. I felt like I had birthed a demon child.

I know that when children are little they tend to not know right from wrong, but then there comes a time when a child gets older. She would initially lie about little things, like eating up the food and drinking up everything. My daughter was always selfish and thought about herself. She has lied to her friends. That is why she no longer has any of those friends.

My daughter has always been a wayward child. I see my daughter as being a part of "…a stubborn and rebellious generation; a generation that did not set its heart aright, and whose spirit was not faithful to God" (Psalm 78:8 NKJV). If I told her to go left, she would go right. If I told her to bring home A's and B's, she would bring home C's on her report card. Sometimes, I believed that she was doing it intentionally.

My daughter would lie to people and tell them that I was not a good mother. Was it that I was not a good mother, or that she was not a good child? People did not know half of what I would go through with that child. I remember going to her elementary school and telling them I have a good twin and a bad twin. Someone said, "Now, mama." I told them, "Well, at least, I am being honest." I used to get calls from just about every school she attended.

As time passed, the lies just kept growing and progressed from one year to another. The lies continued getting worse. As a mother, what do you do?

Mom, what I realized is that there is purpose inside of you that the enemy doesn't want to be released. The enemy is using your wayward child as a distraction. The enemy comes to steal, kill, and destroy. Mom, what is your God-given purpose?

Chapter 1

HER CHILDHOOD

I KNOW THAT WHEN I was little, I was not an angel, but I did have a conscience. When I was little, I told lies. I did not tell the lies that hurt people. My conscience was so intact that when I did lie, I was repentant and remorseful. Don't get me wrong. I am not justifying lies at all.

I always wanted kids. I would keep other people's children while I was single and childless. While attending college, I remember telling a guy on campus that I wanted to become pregnant. In my last year of college, I became pregnant. The doctor stated that I was going to have my baby in October. Well, I ended up being pregnant with twins. They came earlier than we anticipated. I had only one semester left. While they were still in the hospital recovering, I decided to finish up college. I was blessed to have someone from back home keep them while I successfully finished my college career.

After completing my college education, I had the pleasure of rearing my children. Life was not easy. I had to raise them by myself. I was a single parent mom. I enjoyed being a mother, but I wished that I would have had some help from time to time. I have to admit that it was stressful because of the lack of assistance. I needed support to assist with behavioral issues. Don't get me wrong. My maternal grandmother helped as much as she could. My uncle helped with my son. I am a true believer that it takes a village to raise a child.

Have you ever had a wayward child or a child who told more lies than the truth? You are not alone. My daughter has lied ever since she was the age of three. I remember spanking her for telling lies. I had my daughter write a report on lies and read scriptures to help her spiritual walk. I have yelled at her and tried talking to her. No tactic ever worked in my daughter's case. I told my grandmother that I had tried everything. My grandmother stated that they received beatings from lying. In this day and time, you can only do so much, or they will get you for child abuse. I am sorry to inform you. Time-out does not always work for all disobedient and lying children. I have even tried using positive reinforcement, such as rewards for good behavior. It did not work with her. She liked attention any way she could get it, whether it was good or bad. But most of the time, it was for something bad.

I have always told my children that with a positive action is a positive consequence and with a negative action is a negative consequence. There are some exceptions to that rule, but I still believe in that sage and wisdom that I have imparted to my children. I have always told them that wisdom is knowing that you do not know everything.

My daughter would lie about simple things. I recollect when she went to visit with family members. She told my aunt that she did not eat certain foods. LIE. She told my grandmother that she did not drink water out of the faucet. LIE. I don't know why my daughter felt the need to lie about such things.

My daughter was always being mischievous. I remember when I had to take a test one weekend. One of my colleagues babysat my children. She told me that my daughter would block the television. She would get my daughter to sit down, and she would turn around. Next thing she knew, my daughter would return to her position in front of the television. My daughter kept the other children from watching the television. My daughter always wanted to be in control. When she was in kindergarten, she would hover over the basket of books and give the children at her table the books she wanted them to have.

My daughter was mischievous in school. When she was in kindergarten, she kicked the teacher assistant. Her dad was in town for their kindergarten graduation, and he spanked her behind. We were supposed to be attending a great event just to find out that one of our children had done something so dreadful. How embarrassing! It was during this time that I was threatening to send her to a children's home.

I got the papers and kept them. I came close to filling the papers out. While relocating to another town, I contemplated leaving her there.

She became worse instead of getting better. I remember going to her elementary school and telling them I had one good twin and one bad twin. Someone said, "Now, mama." I told them, "Well, at least, I am being honest." I used to get calls from just about every school she attended. She cheated on a test. I told the teacher to give her a zero to teach her a lesson. While in elementary school, she forged my name on papers. She was disruptive in class. I recall paying a surprise visit to her school. I peered through the window and saw her out of her seat just chatting it up. When she saw me, she sat down and closed her mouth. While she was in middle school, she had to sit with the assistant principal every time her class had a substitute teacher in her classroom.

When my daughter was in the fifth grade, she was accused of being a bully. Because she was such a great computer lab and cafeteria helper, the assistant principal did not think that she was a bully. She spoke of how my daughter had a kind heart. However, she did tease a girl for being kicked out of a high-achieving program. My daughter was in this program as well. She also ended up being kicked out of this program because she continued to make C's on her report card. In that program, you must maintain A's and B's. Boy, was I mad! I just figured that was karma for teasing the other girl.

My daughter told lies in her preteen and teenage years. She has written notes to boys on the bus stating that she wanted to engage in sexual relations with them. When asked about what she wrote, she lied. Every time you asked about something she did, she would tell a lie.

I paid for my daughter to attend a prestigious summer college program. I wanted her to receive a bona fide college experience. Sending her there for less than one-week cost more than my house mortgage. When she arrived home, I asked her to mow the lawn. She stated that the riding lawn mower was not working, so I told her to use the push lawn mower. She said that it was not working either. Now, I had just gotten both of them serviced before she arrived back home. She was just being lazy. Nevertheless, she refused to mow the lawn and decided she was going to leave my house. I spanked her behind because it was not the first time she had done this. Don't you know I spanked her and told her to go ahead to later find out that she accused me of scratching her face? On the way to her great-grandmother's house, she scratched her face and blamed me. It was at this time that she went to go reside with her father. Boy, was he in for a rude awakening?

My daughter was always lazy. When I would ask her to do something, she always had to use the bathroom. She would stay in there a long time. I would have to demand that she come out of the bathroom so that she could help. Her room was always the nastiest in the house. She would combine dirty and clean clothes.

I recall when my daughter went to go stay with her dad. I cleaned up her room. She had a bowl of food on the shelf in her closet. Her clothes were nothing that you would want to give to anyone. They were so filthy. I had to put some gloves on to remove them and throw them into the trash. My daughter would always lie about cleaning up her room even as an adult. Her idea of cleaning up was moving everything into another room, trash under a bed, and/or placing it all in the corner of a room. She and I could not live together peacefully due to her untidiness.

My daughter would lie to family members about me. Who listens to a child? Of course, children are going to lie when they are not getting their way. I allowed her to go with her dad. When my daughter left my house, she went with her father. Her father took her to church to speak with one of my family members. My cousin allowed her to stay with her. She said that she did not want her in the streets. I told her that my daughter left my house with her father, and she should have stayed with him.

Next thing I knew, she ended up with my sister. Well, my sister decided that she wanted to listen to what my daughter had to say about me. I remember when my children's father met my sister to let her keep our daughter. That was short-lived. I heard that my daughter was allowing boys into my sister's apartment and taking pictures of herself in a bathing suit in my sister's apartment. Well, my sister did not keep her long before she found out how she was. Needless to say, my sister hurried up and dropped her off. She dropped my daughter back off at my cousin's house so fast that she forgot to bring all her belongings and did not get out of the car to speak. Needless to say, my sister does not have much to say to my daughter when she sees her now. Before all of that, my sister always wanted to speak with my daughter and listen to her lies. Let's just say it backfired on my sister when she decided to keep her. BINGO! Wow! What a life spanking my sister had to endure!

Then, my cousin kept her again for a while. She and my sister compared notes realizing that my daughter was a habitual liar. Is that something that I already knew as her mother? YES, INDEED! But, no one wanted to listen to me. My cousin mentioned that my grandmother had already informed her before that my daughter told lies. I said, "Now, if my grandmother said it, how much more am I going to say it?" Duh! Needless to say, she wore a butt whooping keeping my daughter. When my daughter disrespected her at a family gathering, I heard that was the fastest my cousin had ever moved. However, I had gone out of town. My family kept calling my phone consistently. Additionally, my cousin did not seem to be getting any financial assistance from my daughter's father. Not new to me. I had already told her not to ask me for one red cent because I did not drop her off at her house. She left with her father. When they asked me what they needed to do with her, I told them to take her to where her father resided. That is what they did.

What people fail to realize is that sometimes, if not at all times, children lie to get what they want. They use emotionalism to manipulate others. If they do not get what they want, they will turn on the adult and say anything to make the adult look bad. They do not care if the adult is their mom, dad, teacher, or any other adult. The sad part is that adults will listen to these manipulative individuals. Don't get me wrong. Some children do tell the truth. How can you believe a child you have never raised or spent time with him or her to know if they are lying or telling the truth? My sister has never kept my children. So, how do you know my daughter? Her dad did not spend time with her until she was a teenager. So, how do you know your daughter? Maybe, some adults believe children because they feel guilty about the fact that they have not been there for the child or children.

When my daughter went to go stay with her dad, the lies continued. Boys would call her dad's phone. She would say that they were her cousins. Some of them were her cousins, but I don't know if all of them were her cousins. Some of these boys would call all times of the night. Her dad was not too happy about that. Not to mention, boys called my phone for her as well. I would ask them for their ages. Let's just say, they were too old for my daughter. When I asked them if they knew how old she was, they would inform me that she had lied about her age. I would always tell those guys her real age and informed them that they needed to leave her alone and not mess up their lives with a criminal charge. I explained the laws of the land to them and informed them that it would be in their best interests not to call her again. They thought that I was the coolest mom ever. I did not want them to mess up their lives fooling with someone who had lied about her age and said that she was older than she was.

I remember when a young man gave her a ride, and she told him she was going to give him some gas money. She told the boy she would be right back. She left the boy without paying him the money. The boy asked my son for the money. I told my son that he does not have to pay for his sister's debts. I told my son that I was not going to pay him. I was holding my daughter accountable. At least, I thought I was. She never paid the kind young man the gas money she vowed. I told my son that my daughter has to learn from her actions. Little did I know, this was an indicator of what her adult life was going to resemble.

She and a family member got into an argument about them supposedly telling lies on the other one. The disagreement became physical. It's funny how, when I am raising her, she is an angel. When my daughter showed her true colors, individuals wanted to discuss my daughter with me. While I was trying to set boundaries, everybody thought that I was wrong as a mother. As the old folks used to say, let's just say some people got a taste of their own medicine.

My daughter always liked to be involved in drama. I remember one time I went to pick her up. She was defending her friend and acting in an unsophisticated manner. I told her to get her behind in the car and close her mouth. Now, she was good at taking up for her brother. I did not mind that as much. Siblings need to stick together. However, I felt as though she needed to mind her business when it came to other people's affairs.

I recollect an incident when my daughter was 16 years old. I went to retrieve her from my cousin's house. First of all, I told my cousin not to let my daughter come to her house. I went to go get my daughter to take her home. She refused to go home. She was about to get into the car with another female and her children. The young lady asked my daughter, "What are you getting me mixed up in?" I have respect for that young lady because she told my daughter to listen to her mother. The young lady told my daughter that she could not go with her and left. After she left, my daughter and I got into a heated argument. She was being disobedient and rebellious. She told me she wasn't going with me. Ultimately, I ended up putting her in a headlock and telling my son to call the police. The police came and talked to her. They told her that she could become emancipated from me. They informed her that by the time that happened, she would probably be 18 years old. They also told her that she had to do what I said because she is a minor. Additionally, they informed her that they could take her to jail if I wanted them to do so. They let her know that I was making a great sacrifice to drive her across state lines early in the morning for her to attend school. The officers told her that they would not have driven her across state lines for her to attend the early college program. When my daughter informed the officers that I would not sign the papers for a parent college loan, they informed her that they worked their way through college and paid for their college education. When I was talking to her about making good grades, she did not want to listen. To this day, I am so glad that I did not put my signature on a parent loan for her. She stayed on academic probation, and she has to pay the money back with no Bachelor's degree. I figured I would at least make certain that she received her Associate's degree by taking her across state lines to the early college program. My daughter has lied and told people that she received her Bachelor's degree. She does have her Associate's degree, but not her Bachelor's degree. I do not say that to dishonor her, but to denote her lying tongue.

When she attended the early college program, I was called. My daughter was misbehaving in class. I told her that she better get back in that classroom and keep her mouth shut. Needless to say, I also told her that when she was in middle school. She thought that she was going to change classes. According to her, it was the teacher. As her mother, I knew that it was her. I know that my daughter loves to talk and stick her nose in where it does not belong. I showed up one day unexpectedly to find her out of her seat running her mouth. When she saw me peering through the window into the room, let's just say she found some sense. She sat down and kept her mouth shut. I have always told my children that you cannot learn if you are talking while the teacher is talking. In the Bible, it states, "So then, my beloved brethren, let every man be swift to hear, slow to speak…" (James 1:19 NKJV).

I remember when my daughter attended the early college program. My daughter was always smart in school. It was just that she had book sense, but no common sense. She called me one day stating that she needed money for graduation. Then, she stated that they would not allow her to graduate because she had to take another class. She took the class that summer and finished. Thank God! It was time for her to be on her own with all her lies, manipulation, and drama.

Chapter 2

TEENAGE PREGNANCY

WHAT PEOPLE FAIL TO REALIZE is that lies hurt others emotionally and make a lasting impression. With my daughter, there were no little white lies. I think I could live with the little white lies, but it is the big lies that affect your life and the lives of others that are dangerous. My daughter told colorful lies with vivid details that made you want to believe her. She was good at selling people dreams.

While attending college, my daughter became pregnant. I had a young man whom I did not know contact me on social media. One of the worst things that could happen to a mother is to find out through social media that your daughter is pregnant. Of course, when I found out, I tried to contact her. She avoided me like the plague. However, it was time for her to come home for the holidays, and she needed a place to stay.

There was massive confusion associated with my daughter's pregnancy. When my daughter was pregnant with my grandson, so many of my family members told me to have her get an abortion. I told them, "I love family, but [forget] family." Needless to say, I effectively got my point across. I even told her grandmother that the only thing she would do is get pregnant again. My daughter was unrestrained and boy crazy. I thank God that she did not have a child before then as much as boys called her dad's and my phone. She always lied to the guys about her age. Furthermore, my daughter had the wrong mentality. She thought, like many of us have thought when we were young and dumb, that a baby would keep a man. Having a baby deters a man from being with you.

When my daughter was pregnant with my grandson and there was more than one possibility, people kept telling me that we needed to go on the Maury show. Initially, she had me thinking that there was only one possibility. Well, I talked to one possibility and found out about another possibility. She had been lying to both of them about not seeing the other guy.

In the meanwhile, she was harassing one of the guys while attending college and telling him that he was the father. She went to his dormitory room and caused a big scene. Her father and I were contacted. I called the guy on the phone and told him to give the phone to my daughter. Needless to say, I yelled at her and told her to get her behind out of his room. Not only that, but she also had other people contacting him telling him to take care of his child.

After my grandson was born, the one guy she kept saying was the father had to deal with her drama. I told the guy who was supposed to be the father to get a DNA test. I know. What kind of mother am I? The kind who also has a son and knows that her daughter tells lies. I would not want a female to do that to my son. Over the years, there have been several men who have supported children who did not belong to them. They did not take a DNA test and/or failed to appear in court. Then, they end up resenting the mother and child. You have some guys who go ahead and accept the child because they have taken care of the child since birth.

When I found out that the one she harassed was not the father, I texted him. Jokingly, I informed him that Maury called and said that he was NOT the father. I knew that he was relieved. I was happy that he was not the father because I did not want him to have to deal with my daughter. However, I did want him to be my grandson's dad. He was a great guy. He and I still have a good relationship; however, he avoids my daughter like the plague. Those people who were on her side do not seem to deal with her anymore. I wonder why.

My daughter had told the other possible father that she had an abortion. Needless to say, guess whose baby it ended up being? Ironically, the one whom she told she had an abortion was the father. The one whom she thought was the father was not the father. In the Bible, it says, "Be not deceived; God is not mocked: for whatever a man sows, that he will also reap" (Galatians 6:7 NKJV). Needless to say, she had to hear about that every time she talked to the father about financial assistance and him paying child support. I had to inform him that regardless of her lies my grandson still needed to be taken care of properly.

The lies did not stop there. One day, she even told the father that my grandson was sick and that she had to take him to the doctor. What mother lies about her child being sick? Why would you want to lie on your child like that?

While I was out of town, an older woman told me that family only wants to gossip about your business. She also told me to get my daughter. She said that if your daughter gets pregnant, they will not help. She told the TRUTH. When my daughter had my grandson, no one was knocking down my door to keep him or financially assist with him.

I recall declaring that whoever talked about me as a mother needs to help my daughter take care of her child. One individual stated, "My plate is full." Was she culpable of talking about me as a mother? I know that she was not there to help my daughter financially with my grandson and did not keep him at all. That is why people need to let you rear your children the way you need to rear them. God blessed me with my daughter for a reason. I can deal with my daughter better than anyone because I know her well. I know the true person. Everyone else sees the façade.

In my daughter's teenage and college years, she always had something negative to say about me. When she was in college, she thought that I was supposed to keep my grandson while she finished college. She wanted us to be like other families. However, the other families consisted of two parents. I was a single parent mom, and I was tired after rearing my children. I felt as though it was time for me to live my life for a change. Even though I did not keep my grandson daily, I would keep him often on the weekends. Come to find out, she was still bad mouthing me. Why? Is it because I would not allow you to borrow any money when you have not paid me back? Is it that I am supposed to keep your child so that you can run around and do what you want to do when I have already raised my children? Is it because I do not believe the lies you tell because you have told so many?

My daughter has always spoken badly about me as a mother, but she always needed my help. A situation arose where she and another young lady were supposed to room together. Everybody was supposed to have their money together. Come to find out. Nobody had their money ready, but it was too late. I had already gotten the U-Haul and moved their belongings. I ended up paying both parties' rent and deposit. The other young lady and my daughter were supposed to pay me back. Ask me if I have seen the fruit of that labor. NEGATIVE.

She hoodwinked me on another occasion. When I got ready to move her again, she claimed she had the money to move. When I got there, guess who ended up footing the bill? That's right. ME. I had to rent the U-Haul and provide the gas. She claimed that the bank she does business with was robbed and had frozen her account. Did I forget to mention that I have worked at a bank before? Did she think that I did not know any better? Did she not know that you can go to another branch of the same bank and withdraw funds?

I found out later that the energy company charged me $150 because she did not pay her light bill. Needless to say, I got that money back. I was there when she cashed the check and held my hand out for the $150 she owed me. I was charged on my light bill because I agreed to be her guarantor (co-signer). Boy, did I get gypped? If someone would do that to his/her mother, what makes you think that they would not do it to anyone else?

I remember another instance when my daughter rented a duplex. She did not pay her light bill. So, her lights were disconnected. For a while, she and my grandson were going next door during the day and spending the night in the duplex with no lights. She claimed that she was going to receive financial aid. Listening to her and believing her, I told her to go ahead and pay her bills in advance for a few months. Did I tell you that she lied again? She tried to stay on campus with some of her friends. She ended up having to withdraw and move back home. The campus officials did not allow her to stay on campus with my grandson. My daughter staying on campus with my grandson was against their policy. I was not mad at them because rules are rules.

What do you do as a parent? Were these the generational curses that pastors spoke about? I recall someone saying that your children are much worse than you are in those negative areas of your life. I know that parents love when grandchildren are born because the grandchildren provide their children with payback from what they did to their parents. Needless to say, I told some lies, but not like my daughter.

Chapter 3

ADULTHOOD

THE LIES PROGRESSED FROM ONE year to another and worsened. As my daughter grew older, the spirits of manipulation and poverty added to the existing spirits of lying, control and deception that had attached themselves to my daughter. Some of my daughter's problems were that she hung around the wrong people. My daddy used to say that you were guilty by association. She would allow the wrong people to speak into her ears. They would mislead and misinform her. She did not realize that the enemy was using those wrong voices to keep her from her blessings and destiny.

She would always become impoverished due to her own foolishness and bad decision making. Who would she call? Her brother and me. When she was broke, she would blow up our phones and want us to help her. Being the giving people that we are, we would help. I would help because I always thought about my grandson. My son would help just being that brother with a good heart.

When she was on top of the world and had money, she did not know us. Let's not talk about when tax time came. She was missing in action. You could not tell her anything. She would hang around and help her so-called friends. When she hit rock bottom again, she would contact her brother and me to help her out. But, it comes a time when you must not enable your family members and let them suffer at the hands of their foolish ways. In the Bible, it states, "The fear of the Lord is the beginning of knowledge: but fools despise wisdom and instruction" (Proverbs 1:7 NKJV). You have to gain the mentality to empower people, not enable them. My daughter would continue to walk around in the wilderness, just like the Israelites. My grandmother always said that a hard head makes a soft behind. Some people just have to learn the hard way. My daughter was one of those people.

Now, I will give credit where credit is due. One time, she did pay us back with her tax money. We were grateful for that time that she did pay us back. However, you do know that she came back months later to ask for more money. My son and I knew it was too good to be true.

As a parent, what do you do? I had to learn to put her on the Potter's wheel to let God deal with her. I prayed for my daughter. In the Bible, it says, "Train up a child in the way he should go, And when he is old he will not depart from it" (Proverbs 22:6 NKJV). As I prayed, I remember the Holy Spirit told me to "let her go." Well, I did for a while, but then I picked her back up. I tried to do what only God could do. When I got tired of dealing with her once again, the Holy Spirit let me know that I was enabling her and that I needed to give her to Him. That is just what I did. God dealt with her. However, she was a work in progress. She was still gossiping and lying. I did not understand why a person would want to lie so much. One thing that I learned about my daughter is that she will avoid you when she tells a lie and/or owes you some money.

My grandmother always said, "If you'll lie, you'll cheat. If you'll cheat, you'll steal." My daughter was about to be prosecuted. She said she was not the culprit. I did not put anything past her. My daughter and another person had a situation where the other person had taken some money out of my daughter's account through the ATM and was writing checks on her account. I did not know who to blame. One was an infamous criminal with a rap sheet. The other lied so much I did not know what to believe. When I saw the evidence, I knew my daughter was not lying that time and was not culpable.

I always told my daughter that the tongue she uses to speak about me would be the same tongue that rises against her. When people and her friends started seeing how much she lied, they cut her off. They loved me. Why? I was honest. I helped rectify situations when my daughter did them wrong. They told me all the lies that my daughter had stated about me. I even told one person that I was waiting for her call. It was just a matter of time. When people saw my daughter for who she was, they stopped dealing with her. My daughter does not have friends. She has acquaintances who discover that her truths are actually lies and then they disassociate themselves with her. My daughter has lost countless friends because of her lies.

She had one friend who helped her get a phone and did not want to pay her. This friend got her a phone and placed her on her line. My daughter decided she did not want to pay the bill. She also avoided her in giving her back the phone. The young lady threatened to file charges. I told her that I would not be mad if she did. My daughter was wrong. How could you wrong the same friend who kept your child and included you in her bridal party? Mind you, she was a part of this friend's bridal party about a year before. She lied even then about being with her friend celebrating her at her bridal shower that weekend. Instead of attending her son's game, she pretended to be with this friend who was getting married. Come to find out, she was still in town hanging out with family. She could have attended her child's game the next morning and rode with us to the out of town wedding. To God be the glory! As my grandson and I headed to the wedding, she called. Lo and behold, she was stuck at a store due to car troubles. The car had overheated. Ironically, we just happened to be approaching that exit. Look at God! How is it that you were nowhere near your friend's wedding location? She kept lying. She said that she had to go and pick up some shoes. I never saw those shoes. She asked me to go and find her some shoes. I could not find any. They improvised. I was doing good to get her to the wedding on time. By the way, I helped her pay for that car. She was supposed to pay me back. Ask me if I have seen a dime of that money. You guessed it. No! Not to mention, she never went back to retrieve the car. Months later, I went back to the location to find the car gone.

While she was in college, she had friends whom I no longer see. She had a great landlord that was kind enough to help her get a car by getting a car loan. She told us that she bought her new car with her good credit. Come to find out someone else had gotten the car for my daughter and required my daughter to make the payments. When she would go to retrieve the payment, my daughter would give her $17 when the car payment was $150. She would also tell her that she had not cashed her check. She almost had my son and me feeling sorry enough to pay her car payment, but God is good. I received a phone call from a woman who left a message on my phone stating that she was going to press charges, if my daughter did not pay her for the car. Needless to say, I called her back to discover more lies. My daughter had this woman thinking that she had returned home to assist me. What lies! I had to help the landlord get the car keys back so that she could confiscate the car. They saw her for the compulsive liar that she was in their lives. She told lies similar to Jacob in the Bible. I said to God, "I need for you to turn her into Israel." I had to pray that God would help me to see her as He sees her. Honestly, I was not seeing it.

When Christmas would come around, she would talk about all the things she would buy my older grandson. I, trying to make certain that he had a great Christmas, would buy what she claimed she was going to buy. When we would go out of town or plan to do something, there was always something wrong with her bank card. I recall when it was time for her to move, something was wrong with her card. I also recall when she had my older grandson. She said that she was going to receive scholarship monies. I told her to pay her rent and bills with that money. She had to live off-campus because they did not accommodate family situations. Well, she lied. She ended up getting evicted out of the duplex she was renting. I was not about to take care of two households. I had already paid the rent for a couple of months.

I believe that my daughter's life was just a lie. My son always said that he thought that his sister lived in a fantasy world. I am starting to believe in his philosophy. One year, she lied about buying her son gifts for Christmas and his birthday. One of her associates confirmed that the guy she was seeing went and bought my grandson's Christmas gifts. I had already thought that he did before she confirmed it. The guy she was seeing even called me before Christmas and asked me about my grandson's sizes since I appeared to be more knowledgeable about his sizes than my daughter—his mom.

She also said that her boyfriend was coming down to meet her father and me to ask for her hand in marriage. Needless to say, we never saw him. She did not arrive at my house for Christmas until that afternoon. Don't you think she should have arrived that morning since her son was with his Nana? She also said that her boyfriend was coming to her son's birthday party, but he was a no show once again. Was the relationship just in her mind?

I believe that one of the guys she was in a relationship with would have married her, but she did not keep a clean house. My daughter would always claim that she was cleaning her house. When you arrived, it would be filthy and messy. I did not know what my daughter's idea of cleanliness was, but it was not applesauce on the floor for about a week. It was also not syrup on the floor for weeks either. She would take items and stuff them in her son's room. It was more of a storage room than my grandson's room. When she was younger, she professed to clean up at her dad's house. When I went to her room, I saw drawers on the floor and clothes everywhere.

She started becoming more creative with her lies. They were not little white lies, but lies that hurt deep to the soul. They were the kind of lies that were destroying the world of those around her. She was not only lying to me, her mother, but her son and her brother. She had lied to people who have tried to help her and to everyone whom she has come in contact with over her lifetime.

It all began when my daughter said that she was having twins. Now, I believed what she was saying because she had already had one child. I told my family the news believing her to end up looking like a fool.

One morning, she texted me stating that she was having the twins and to send up a prayer. While my son and I were getting close to the place where she lived, I called the hospital to make certain that she was there. They said that they did not have any records of my daughter. Later on, I found out that the supposed twins' father went to the hospital and found out that they had no record of my daughter as well. Likewise, her former landlord received the same text that the rest of us did.

Now, I spoke with my daughter before I left home. She informed me that she had to talk quickly because the anesthesiologist was going to be gone for two minutes and that she was not supposed to be on the phone. Keep in mind that I took off work, and my son missed an interview. When we texted her to find her location, she informed us that she was in another town. She was texting from her phone pretending to be one of her friends. My daughter was texting several people pretending to be someone else. Does my daughter have multiple personalities? That same day, my daughter was texting me pretending to be a girl named Ashley. She was saying that she did not want to get in the middle of what was going on. It was at that moment that we were told that the supposed children's father had gotten married. Eventually, my daughter was texting saying that he had made his decision a long time ago and that she was just trying to make him look good. That is when I informed her that she was not fooling anyone. We already knew better. Pretending to be Derius, she texted her former landlord that she was alright. Talk about a web of lies. My dad always told us to tell the truth. He said that if you tell a lie, you will have to come up with more lies to cover the other lies. Not to mention, you have to remember the lies you told so you will not get caught in your lies.

My son and I went to the wrong town. When we got back on track, she was not at the hospital. With the help of the Holy Spirit, we both concluded that we needed to go back to the town where she lived. When we arrived, we saw where the door was open. We went in to speak with her. She informed us that she had the twins a month ago. That same day, she claimed that a doctor and lawyer couple adopted the twins.

So, we talked to her and listened to her. We consoled her, and let her know that we were there for her. We showed her some love, grace, and mercy. After we left, we got to thinking that several things she said did not add up.

I called the proposed twins' father. He informed us that she said that she was having twins that day. He also confirmed an earlier text that she had sent stating that he had gotten married. Wow, news to us! Before all of this, she was talking about how she and the proposed twins' father were supposed to get married. She also talked about how he was going to pay for all the bills. She had my family believing her lies. My son and I knew better. She would tell me that the proposed father would not attend prenatal appointments with her, but he said that she would tell him that the appointments were canceled. He also stated that she sent him a copy of a sonogram, but his sister said that the sonogram did not look similar to those sonograms presented in their county. He hinted that my daughter sent him a fake sonogram from the Internet. Before he mentioned that to us, I had already told my son that she probably got it off the Internet. After we talked to him, we were all in agreement that my daughter was lying and something just was not adding up.

We convinced her to come home, and the lies worsened. She told us that she had a Cesarean section. My son said that he did not see an incision on her stomach because I had him look it up on the Internet to educate himself on what a Cesarean section incision should look like. My son realized that after a few days of my daughter staying with him that he could not take her staying there. So, he informed her that she had to go. Well, she told him that she was going to take my grandson to a shelter. She said that she had spoken to someone, and the representative told her that he had to be there by a certain time. LIE. You forgot that your mother volunteered at that same shelter. They take children at any time of the day and night.

I looked in retrospect. When she came to my house one weekend during her proposed pregnancy, I noticed that her stomach jiggled. When a woman is pregnant, the stomach has a firm shape. I asked her if she was pregnant and how much did the twins weigh. She said that they weighed about one pound around seven months of her alleged pregnancy. Now, how is it that you told me you were due in December, but you are at seven months in September? You do the math. She also told me that the twins went home after being in the hospital for one month. Now, I am a mother of twins who were premature and underweight by about three pounds. My son came home after a month of being in the hospital, and my daughter came home after a month and a half of being in the hospital. To leave the hospital, babies must weigh approximately five pounds. How is it that babies around one pound get to leave the hospital after a month of being there? That does not sound right medically or logically. Who does she think I am—Boo Boo the Fool?

After months of still trying to figure out what was the truth and what was a lie, we discovered that she was lying altogether about birthing the twins. What a web of lies she told! She had me in an emotional state. I thought that I had grandbabies out there somewhere, but found out that she was telling a lie. She had me looking like a fool to my family. I concluded that she just wanted attention. Ironically, the truth was revealed when she had my younger grandson. The timing did not add up. My grandson came on time, so there was no way two pregnancies overlapped. My dad always told us to tell the truth because you have to remember the lies you told.

The one time I decided to trust my daughter I shouldn't have. Whoever would have thought that my daughter would have told these types of lies? I felt like a fool believing her. I took off from work believing that she was having my twin grandbabies to be considerably disappointed.

The hurtful lies did not stop there. She stated that she went to the doctor and had blood clots near her heart. My son was dating a girl who informed him that blood clots near the heart were life-threatening. My son cried because he thought that his sister was going to die. We were on the phone trying to determine how we would raise my grandson. Being the inquisitive mother that I am, something did not sit right. I researched the prescriptions that the doctor had prescribed her. Come to find out the medications were for nausea. She had us thinking that she was about to die. My daughter always came up with some bizarre lies. How does one lie like that?

At this point, I had started to believe that my daughter had mental issues and needed mental health services. After speaking to a mental health counselor, she confirmed that her actions were behavioral and that she just had self-esteem issues. My daughter's ex-boyfriend and I talked. He told me that my daughter wanted to be like me, but she was going about it the wrong way. I did notice that she would talk about going on cruises, getting her Master's degree, and becoming a teacher amongst other things. However, I did not realize how much she wanted to be like me until she said that she was having boy-girl twins. I had boy-girl twins. Coincidence? I don't think so. Honestly, I felt like she wanted to compete with me at times. I remember when one of the possible fathers told her she should be cool like me. I reiterated what he said. She said, "Why don't you be with him then?" How ludicrous!

My daughter talked about getting her Master's degree. Well, she needed to get her Bachelor's degree first. She was posting on social media that she was graduating. My family was contacting me. I told them that I would believe it when I saw it. My family thought that I was wrong in my statements about my daughter. What they did not know is that my daughter would claim that she was making good grades in college. Then, she told everyone, whom she associated with, that she finished her degree through online classes. Boy, did she fool everyone! I remember when I was receiving failure notices and academic probation notices for probably every semester she attended college. She even told her former landlord that she was graduating on a certain day and that she had no one to support her. The landlord said that she would attend. My daughter proceeded to say that she would not be attending her graduation. Later on, she told her landlord that she went ahead and participated in the graduation ceremony, but did not invite her. Ask any of us if we have ever seen her Bachelor's degree? See how a person has to keep telling lies to cover the other lies?

My daughter proclaimed that she wanted to start her own business. I supported her venture. I remember when my daughter claimed that she was going to meet with a millionaire and receive $500,000. Every time, it was time to take a family trip. She had a "meeting" with the millionaire. Well, what happened to the money? We never saw the fruit of the meeting. She continued to be destitute. We never saw the business she was supposed to start.

Supposedly, she started before I did. So, tell me why I am ahead of her on the business venture God had for me. What I have learned about my daughter is that she is a follower. She wants to be like other people, but she does not want to put in the work. I recall her telling me that she was going to go to the courthouse to open up her LLC. I informed her that you have to apply to the Secretary of State. Wow! I wonder how she felt at that moment of being caught in a lie.

On another occasion, my daughter was supposed to take the kids to the beach. She had us thinking that she went, but my granddaughter went back to her mom's house and said that they did not go to the beach. She did not take the kids to the beach and told them that the beach was closed. We kept calling and texting her phone. My daughter made it seem as though she was stressed and didn't know if she was going to get her money back from the hotel she booked. She claimed that they shut everything down from the coronavirus. She texted me talking about curfews, places being shut down, and people staying in the house.

She and my grandchildren were supposed to come and visit with me. She let me know that she did not know if they were going to be able to come. It made me wonder if she booked the flight? Well to her advantage, the flight was canceled due to the COVID-19 pandemic.

My daughter had another phone incident. She borrowed a phone from someone. My son tried to retrieve the phone. She hid from my son like he was a bill collector. She even claimed that she had to walk to work. Did you walk over 45 miles to work? I don't think so. Like my son stated, "She might have walked to [a local fast food restaurant], but she did not walk to work." My daughter's lies became more creative as she continued to tell them. How do you walk to work and then you arrive at home after midnight? How is it when your brother comes to retrieve an item, you say that your babysitter did not feel comfortable answering the door? Really? I think that you were hiding like people do when the bill collector comes, and you don't have the money.

My daughter would fool people initially. When they saw her true colors, they would side with me. My daughter always tried to be manipulative. She always deflected instead of reflecting. It was always everybody else's fault and not her own. My daughter loved to play on people's emotions. I remember when she had moved to a different town. A woman there would keep my grandson. Finally, she got tired of my daughter. I had been through so much with my daughter that by the time she called I remember saying to her, "I was wondering when you were going to call." She told me that she used profanity with my daughter and saw why I was the way I was. She informed my daughter that I was not the problem, but let my daughter know that she was the problem.

She has borrowed money from people and not paid it back. I have also had to retrieve a phone that one of her friends helped her get because she did not want to pay her. Instead of paying her as they had verbally agreed upon, she avoided her. I liked this friend. My daughter always had great friends. She just wasn't a good friend to others. Once I finally got my daughter to see how wrong she was, I returned the phone to her friend. Sadly, a good friendship ended. I still like the other young lady. She has never done anything to me. I was always cleaning up my daughter's messes.

My daughter continued to make poor decisions. She would run after guys who were not good for her. I remember when she was running after some guy who was unemployed and entertaining other women.

He tried to convey to me that he had a job. I knew he was lying when he said it. My daughter would hype him up. She lied and said that he was working for his mom. How ironic! When I went to stay at my daughter's apartment for a few days during the holidays, he seemed to be at the apartment more than I was. Not only that, but he was consuming the oatmeal and snacks I bought for my grandchildren. When I brought my grandchildren back home with me, I brought the snacks back too. This young man ended up getting into some trouble. My daughter had some money and ended up spending it on this guy leaving her penniless. How did you go through so much money so quickly? Good things do not come to people who do people wrong. What's sad is that she went through a substantial amount of money in a short time with someone who did not mean her any good. Afterward, she went to donate bone marrow for money. I'm not judging anyone, but I just could not see myself giving up a part of me for money. Ask my daughter where that guy is now.

Around the same time, she lied about moving. She tried to say that she was moving on her own free will. Later on, I found out that she was evicted. My daughter was evicted on several occasions. Every time she would get evicted, she would leave the children's clothes, toys, and furniture behind. I never understood her way of thinking.

My daughter had the worst relationship with guys. One guy hit on her. The other guys were always on the passenger side when I would meet her to get my grandson. She would get with guys and run up and down the highway to get them. Where were their cars? I remember when my son told me that one of the guys said he made $900 a week. I asked my son why he did not have a car. My son had to ponder over it. He finally comprehended what I was trying to tell him. If he made that much money a week, he should have had a car.

What I observed with my daughter is that she enjoys the wilderness. She reminds me of the Israelites walking through the wilderness for 40 years when the time could have been shortened. I wonder when my daughter is going to change and be transformed by the renewing of her mind. Is she going to die in the wilderness or see her Promised Land?

Chapter 4

PARENTING

MY IDEAS OF PARENTING AND my daughter's ideas of parenting varied. Just because you have a child doesn't make you a mother. I know that my daughter was a teenage mother. I tried to provide her with sage and wisdom, but she was so rebellious. She thought that giving a child life, some clothes, and halfway putting a roof over your child's head makes you a good parent. I don't know what world my daughter was living in.

I would always tell my daughter to put her kids first. When my first grandson was born, my daughter stayed with me. She would stay in the backroom and consistently be on the phone. As much as I would tell her to spend time with my grandson, she wouldn't. She thought that playing ball with my grandson was futile. I let her know that it was referred to as bonding. I guess that's part of the reason why my grandson and I have a strong bond now. Not to mention, I have kept him at times so that she could get herself together.

My daughter has countlessly lied to my grandson. Sometimes, I think that he was confused as to what was a lie and what was the truth. She would tell him that she was going to put him in sports. One time, she claimed that she tried to sign him up for football. She told him and me that there were not enough participants. Tell me why my grandson's teacher coached the cheerleaders and my cousin's grandson was on a team. On the day of Grandparent's Day, the kids were walking around with their jerseys on. Was she lying about that too? After conversing with her again, she was still claiming that same lie. I believe that she just did not have the money.

I would have paid for it. When I paid for my grandson to play football, my daughter did not seem to care about getting him to practice or the games. Why should she? She was not paying for it. As a parent, my daughter was so irresponsible. They would get evicted from places. She seemed to enjoy staying in shelters. She had cars repossessed. Her lights would be turned off. When she had a place of residence, it was filthy. I would find trash and dirty diapers under the bed. All she liked to do was sit on her behind, eat, be on her phone, and bark orders at my older grandson.

My daughter has lied to my grandson about what she was going to do. My older grandson visited me for a month. Oh, she claimed that she was going to work overtime. She was staying at home, just as much as I was. She was supposed to bring her younger son to enjoy the amusement park with us in Florida. It was my older grandson's birthday. All she had to do was spend approximately $100. It was a buy one get one free. Instead, all she did was pick up the older son causing my younger grandson to miss out. My older grandson wanted his brother there with him to enjoy the amusement park.

She was penniless again asking her brother for money and didn't desire to pay him back. She avoided him like he was a bill collector. When will she see the error of her ways?

Before that moment, she lied and said that she had taken a day off work. How is it Tuesday, and you say that you start back to work on Friday? Does that make any sense? When she knew that I was coming into town, she admitted that she lied and quit her job. One day, I heard someone cursing my daughter out. She lied to the boy because she did not have gas in her car to pick her older son up from school. The school was only five minutes away. That is what happens when you quit your job, and don't have a plan. Sweetheart, you can't be like your mother. Mama has saved up for a time such as this. Remember when the Lord showed Potiphar the seven years of abundance and the seven years of famine.

My daughter was just like Joseph's brothers. She meant evil against me, but God meant it for my good (Genesis 50:20 NKJV). It sounds like deja-vu. How ironic! During her time of unemployment, my grandson became sick. She could not even purchase any over-the-counter remedies for his ailment. My grandmother always told us to save at least $5 out of every check. When emergencies arose, you would have money saved.

To put the icing on the cake, she claimed that she had a new job. How is it that you say you work for a company where you were in arrears on your electric bill? You must think that your mother is a fool. I know they had to check your credit. Why lie? Just say that you do not have a job. I let her think that I believed her and texted her, "Congratulations!" I wanted her to see me as a supportive mother.

After the birth of my younger grandson, the lies did not get any better. Here we go back to the wilderness moments. She was like the Israelites. She wanted the familiar. She loved Egypt and the wilderness. The imprisonment of the mindset was the story of her life. She enjoyed telling lies. My daughter has lied about getting her younger son. She would tell me that the reason she was not getting him was because his dad and his family had plans. When I would talk to them, it was that she was supposed to get him. They would call her countless times and could not reach her. She would call after she was supposed to take him back and tell her son that she loved him.

I would continuously tell my daughter to get my younger grandson. She would not listen. His dad was keeping him and paying her child support. I instructed her to drop the child support. She would say, "Ok." Weeks would pass by, and she still did not comply. She tried to go to court and get her child's father for child endangerment. She was so determined to allow the dad to keep their son that she let him keep him after a detrimental situation occurred between them. It made the judge question her motives and intentions. Well, karma hit. She enjoyed being in control until an incident happened to where God let her know that He was in control by allowing the judge to rule against her on the guardianship of her younger son. That's right. His dad was granted sole custody of my grandson. What a blow! Afterward, she lied to my older grandson by telling him that my younger grandson was only staying with his dad for a year. I told my grandson the truth about the situation. I sensed that he would have figured it out even if I would not have told him.

My daughter did not want to listen to me. She always knew more than me and every other wise voice that attempted to speak to her. She was and is one who believes that she does not do anything wrong and that her stuff does not stink. Sound familiar? There are times when we do not want to read the Bible because it shows us who we are and who we are not. Are you saved? Are you living for God? Do you have a relationship with God? "There is a way which seems right to a man, But its end is the way to death" (Proverbs 14:12 NKJV).

When she was supposed to get her son for visitation, she told her younger son's father that her dad had a light stroke and that is why she could not pick up her son. Did she visit her dad, and for how long? She could have picked up her son. Is it that she did not have any gas money? Tell me why my daughter could not see the error of her ways. She even lied and claimed that there was traffic of countless people in and out of my younger grandson's grandmother's house. When I spoke to the dad, he refuted the allegations. Who do you think that I believed? His dad. Sorry, young people. When you continuously tell lies, no one believes you. Your parents desire to trust you, but you provide them with reasons not to trust you. When something significant and relevant happens, you wonder why they are in disbelief. It is because you have lied one too many times. I'm just shaking my head. I have to ask others to make certain that what my daughter is saying is the truth. I have to get it in black and white print.

I don't understand how someone can tell so many lies. On another occasion, my daughter had to go pick up her younger son at the meeting point. She called me and asked me to cash app her gas money. I told her that I would when I arrived at my destination. When I arrived, she called back and proclaimed that she had found $20 in the car. Later, I found out that she could not start her car. The car was empty. So, her younger son's paternal grandmother went to go get her some gas. Then, she provided my daughter with some gas money. My grandson's grandmother could not bear to see them on the side of the road. What's ironic is that you can travel up and down the road to pick up a grown male but not have enough gas to pick up your son every other weekend. What's wrong with that picture?

On Christmas, she did not have any gifts for my grandsons. The expressions on their sweet, little faces reaped in disappointment. Thank God, they went with their dads for the rest of that Christmas day to receive their gifts. She lied and told them that she ordered their bikes and said that they were not delivered on time. I told her that Christmas comes at the same time every year. My daughter is so selfish. The younger grandson told his dad that he felt sad that his mom did not get him anything for Christmas. How would that make you feel as a mother? Even an inexpensive gift from the dollar store would have been better than nothing at all. I thank God that I was able to supply them with some gifts from me. They had an attitude of gratitude.

Is that true parenting? I know that we were not provided with a manual, but I know that I was a better example. I am not saying that I was perfect, but I was selfless and put my kids first.

Chapter 5

RENTING FROM YOUR MOTHER

BEFORE I MOVED TO TEXAS, I allowed my daughter to move in again. Before she moved in, she and my grandchildren had been residing in a shelter. For a while, she was missing in action. She did not speak with her brother or me. As always, she finally came around. By this time, she no longer had her car and was homeless.

When my daughter is down and out, she humbly approaches me. I allowed her and my grandson to move in with me. The other grandson went to go stay with his dad. Things went well for a while. She was paying me for a couple of months to stay there. Usually, I would allow her to stay for free. This time, I thought that she should pay a small fee to teach her some responsibility.

I recall praying to God to inquire about what to do with my house. It was about time for me to move to Texas. On the way from the airport, I heard the Holy Spirit tell me to allow my daughter to stay in my house. I was obedient. I conferred with my daughter and presented a lease agreement to her. My daughter agreed to rent from me. Mind you, she already had a history of evictions. I thought maybe she would do better renting from her mother. Wrong!

Initially, my daughter was doing well paying the rent. All of a sudden, she decided she did not want to pay rent. She was not working and became very disrespectful. The Holy Spirit said, "You are dealing with people with a sense of entitlement."

I guess she thought that I was not going to evict her. She was in for a rude awakening. I sent her some eviction papers. At one point, I thought she had moved. She sent me text messages like she had a place and stated that she and her children were good. Well, how many of you know that was a lie? Come to find out her lights had been disconnected for over a week. I had already wondered if it was voluntarily or involuntarily. My educated guess is that it was involuntary.

When I sent someone out to change the locks, he was only able to change the locks on one of the doors. In the meantime, she went back into the house to stay there. So, has she been staying at the house for over a week with no electricity? How is that being good? You say you work two jobs, and you still can't pay your bills. At least, she claimed that she was working two jobs. Maybe, she was eating up the profits.

To her benefit, I did not serve her eviction papers properly. I ended up having to file eviction papers with the sheriff's office and have them serve her. Wow! Did we not get a revelation after walking around in the same wilderness on an annual basis? Wherever my daughter goes, she does not believe in paying the bills. As a mother, I realized that you have to let your child go and provide him/her with some tough love. They say that experience is the best teacher.

When she did not pay rent, I believed that she was allowing the enemy to use her as a distraction trying to keep me from fulfilling God's purpose for my life. How many know that God will move you half-way across the country to get you away from your family? I kept telling people that it was a female Abraham move. God told me to leave my family, my country, and my property. "For whoever desires to save his life will lose it, but whoever loses his life for My sake will save it" (Luke 9:24 NKJV).

She also proclaimed that an ex she was seeing stated that if he could not have her then no one else could. My daughter has lied so much that I did not know what to believe. My daughter made it seem as though this guy adored her. The last time I saw him, he was cursing her out. If that is the case, why are you not staying with him? Why are your lights off? I'm perplexed. He can't help you, or are you lying again? What is so funny is that I have not seen him in a long time. It must have been a fantasy in her head.

Even though I had my daughter evicted, I prayed that God would provide for her and my grandsons. I did not want them to stay in a shelter again. I know that God heard my prayers. She ended up renting from one of my family members. Initially, I did not like the thought of her renting from a family member. I felt disrespected, but God reminded me of my prayer. I conceded to God's will.

Chapter 6

PRAYING FOR SALVATION

SOMETIMES, I WOULD WONDER WHERE I went wrong. As her mother, I'll have to admit that I am not her only influence. My daughter has a mind of her own. If it was up to her, she would sit on her behind every day, eat, and watch television. Now, those things she was great at doing. I'm surprised she worked at a fast-food restaurant as long as she did. Then again, they did have her favorite thing: food. She was never one to keep a job. Eventually, she walked out on that job. She claimed that they cut her hours. Only God knows.

My daughter and I did not have the best relationship at times. We were both stubborn and head-strong. However, we did have moments where we did get along. I felt like we were experiencing the generational curse that had vexed our family of mothers and daughters not getting along with one another. My mom and my maternal grandmother did not get along. My mom and I did not get along. Then, there was my daughter and me. I wanted that curse to stop with me. Some of my aunts and their daughters did not get along. Some of my cousins and their daughters did not get along. It was rampant in our family line. Some moms and daughters could not live in the same household together due to so much confusion and disagreements among them. When was it going to stop?

While I was sitting in church one Sunday morning, the Lord spoke in my spirit and told me to "let her go." Sometimes, as parents, we have to let our children go and let them learn from their own experiences even though we want to protect them from everything. For the parent dealing with the wayward child, you are not alone. For the parent dealing with the lying child, you are not alone. Sometimes, we feel like we are the only ones going through these ordeals.

At one point, I was fasting, praying, and seeking God on her behalf. I prayed that she would attend a Bible-based church. Well, my daughter eventually began to attend church. Hallelujah! While she was attending church, she was humble and doing better. It seemed as though she was working out her salvation until she arrived at my house after a couple of months. What I learned is that she was like several people. Being church-wise, she went to church when she was downtrodden seeking God. When life got better for her, she left the church. When she thought that she had arrived, she put God down just like she did with her brother and me.

Honestly, I thought that she enjoyed attending that church. What caused her to slip? Is it because she realized that she needed to confess her sins and make some significant changes in her life? Did the pastor step on her toes? Did he see what I saw in my child?

As the mother of such a child, it was frustrating, to say the least. Then I heard a sermon by Pastor Joel Osteen. He talked about speaking God's promises back to Him and declaring, "God you promised me that my children would rise up and call me blessed." I decided to try it to see what the results would be. I learned to trust God. I believed that He was going to do what He said He was going to do. One thing that I love about God is that He is "not a man, that He should lie, Nor a son of man, that He should repent…" (Numbers 23:19 NKJV).

My daughter lied so much. I became frustrated. After God moved me, I prayed about her and her lying. I finally proclaimed to God, "I am so tired of my daughter lying." Next thing I knew, God was telling me to apologize to her. Apologize to her? Little did I know, God's plan was better than any plan I had ever implemented. She listened to my apology. She spoke about how she felt as though I did not love her. I informed her that I did love her. I believed that if I let her back in my house, after her many unsuccessful attempts at life, that was showing her that I loved her. She proclaimed that she did not feel loved because I praised my son. "A wise son makes a glad father, But a foolish son is the grief of his mother" (Proverbs 10:1 NKJV). I apologized and informed her that I didn't mean to make her feel unloved. What I began to learn about my daughter is that to tell her that you love her is her love language. Her dad could say that he loved her and did not do anything for her, and she was good. I did not comprehend that, but everybody has his or her love language. However, I did state the context in which things were said and done. I informed her that she was disrespectful, accosting, and defiant. After the apology, the lies did not stop. She continued to lie. I was told that my daughter possessed the Jezebel spirit. My daughter encompassed the characteristics of the Jezebel spirit, which are deception, manipulation, control, insubordination, feigned repentance, sexual immorality, and pride. Beware of the Jezebel spirit. It comes to steal, kill, and destroy.

After some time, she apologized to me for being so disrespectful. I recollect that day having plans, but I chose to listen. Sometimes, we do not need to be so busy that we do not listen to our children. She discussed how someone said that she was ugly, just like her dad. I did recall that moment. I told her that people took what that person said lightly and as a grain of salt. She also talked about how she was defensive when I spoke to her. She stated how she felt like she had to take care of her brother and do things for him. While I was apologizing for that, she stated that was when she went to stay with her dad. She also discussed her daddy issues. I had already recognized the absence of her father being her primary issue. Even though she stayed with him, it was for a short time. She longed to be a daddy's girl. She was trying to fill a void.

What I learned is that my daughter was a distraction. It was about what God was calling me to do. God was taking me to my purpose.

What is so sad is that I tried to be that supportive mom whom God called me to be. It's difficult to be that supportive mom when you have supported your child to find out that she has lied about her accomplishments. But then, she thinks that you are wrong when you don't support because you do not know if she is telling the truth or not.

I continued to pray for my daughter. The Holy Spirit said that she was "rebellious." As someone with a prophetic gift, I conveyed the message to her. Next thing I knew, I was blocked. It was fine. Maybe God was dealing with her. I was in another state praying for her and asking God to send angels into her room to speak to her. I was also asking God to deal with her heart and mind in addition to convicting her heart.

As I continued to pray for my daughter's salvation, the Holy Spirit said, "She can't go where I am taking you." Wow! What a revelation! I will admit that while I was growing up, I was obstinate at times myself. I rejected toxic information and pondered over beneficial information. "Blessed is the man that walketh not in the counsel of the ungodly, nor standeth in the way of sinners, nor sitteth in the seat of the scornful" (Psalm 1:1 NKJV). My daughter did not read those Bible verses. She kept people around her who spoke the wrong things in her life, including herself. "Death and life are in the power of the tongue: and they that love it shall eat its fruit" (Proverbs 18:21 NKJV).

God had already told me to give her to Him. To Him, I gave her. During the COVID-19 pandemic, I felt like God was doing a work. I was praying that God would turn the hearts of the parents back to the children and the hearts of the children back to the parents (Malachi 4:6 NKJV). During the pandemic, the Holy Spirit instructed me to go home. Reluctantly, I went. Then, I said, "Okay, God. You are right. I don't know when the next time I will be able to go home." The day after Mother's Day, I arrived in my hometown to spend time with my family. My daughter's place of residence was the first place I visited. I said, "Happy Belated Mother's Day!" It was a great Mother's Day gift from God. My daughter was starting to act like someone with some sense. I knew that God had dealt with her. As parents, we have to let go and let God deal with us and our children. We also have to be obedient, loving and nurturing. I also learned that it was good for a parent to show tough love. We try to protect our children from making the same mistakes we made, but they have to experience life for themselves. They have to get to know God for themselves.

My daughter is still a work in progress. My daughter has told so many lies that I don't even think that she can keep up. After visiting with her at home, she told me that she passed a drug test she had to take. Later on, she told me that they did not obtain enough hair for the drug test. Which one is it? If you passed, why do they require more hair?

Children, stop telling lies. What I have found is that lies can hurt. No lie is acceptable. Just tell the truth because the truth will set you free.

"The father of a righteous child has great joy; a man who fathers a wise son rejoices in him" (Proverbs 23:24 NKJV).

Lies can be dangerous. Children, you want your parents to believe you, but you lie. How can your parents trust you? If you lie often, you will be devastated when your parents do not believe you when you need for them to believe and hear you. Children, stop telling lies.

Parents, stop allowing your children to be distractions. God has something greater for you. If the enemy can't get to you, he uses those close to you. The enemy knows that your purpose and ministry will save countless souls for the kingdom of God.

Printed in the United States
By Bookmasters